T0324348

ORANGES AND SNOW

FACING PAGES

NICHOLAS JENKINS

Series Editor

After Every War
Twentieth-Century Women Poets
translations from the German by Eavan Boland

Horace, The Odes
New Translations by Contemporary Poets
edited by J. D. McClatchy

Hothouses
Poems 1889, by Maurice Maeterlinck
translated by Richard Howard

Landscape with Rowers
Poetry from the Netherlands
translated and introduced by J. M. Coetzee

The Night
by Jaime Saenz
translated and introduced by Forrest Gander
and Kent Johnson

Love Lessons: Selected Poems of Alda Merini
translated by Susan Stewart

Angina Days: Selected Poems
by Günter Eich
edited and introduced by Michael Hofmann

Oranges and Snow: Selected Poems of Milan Djordjević
translated from the Serbian by Charles Simic

ORANGES AND SNOW

SELECTED POEMS OF Milan Djordjević

TRANSLATED AND INTRODUCED BY Charles Simic

PRINCETON UNIVERSITY PRESS   Princeton and Oxford

Copyright 2010 © by Princeton University Press

Published by Princeton University Press, 41 William Street, Princeton, New Jersey 08540

In the United Kingdom: Princeton University Press, 6 Oxford Street, Woodstock, Oxfordshire OX20 1TW

press.princeton.edu

Some of the translations of these poems have appeared in the following publications to whose editors a grateful acknowledgment is made: *Field* and *Tri-Quarterly*.

Library of Congress Cataloging-in-Publication Data

Djordjević, Milan, 1954–

  [Poems. English & Serbian. Selections]

  Oranges and snow : selected poems of Milan Djordjević / translated [from the Serbian] and introduced by Charles Simic.

     p. cm. —(Facing pages)

  Parallel Serbian and English text.

  ISBN 978-0-691-14246-3 (cloth : alk. paper) 1. Djordjević, Milan, 1954– —Translations into English. I. Simic, Charles, 1938– II. Title.

  PG1419.14.J69A613 2010

  891.8'216—dc22

                                  2010006052

British Library Cataloging-in-Publication Data is available

This book has been composed in Minion with Myriad

Printed on acid-free paper. ∞

Printed in the United States of America

10 9 8 7 6 5 4 3 2

CONTENTS |

vi

The value of knowing one of the smaller languages of the world and loving literature lies in the discoveries one is likely to make of writers and poets who, despite being astonishingly good, are completely unknown outside of their countries. I can imagine even those who never dreamed of translating a literary work being tempted to do so after reading an extraordinary book or a poem. This is certainly how I started as a translator. Forty-five years ago, I came across a poem by the Serbian poet Vasko Popa in the New York Public Library's Slavic Division, fell in love with it, and had an instant, overwhelming desire to turn it into English and show it to my poet friends. Since one was prohibited from borrowing books from that division of the library, and copy machines were still not widely in use, I wrote the poem in long hand in my notebook and hurried home to see what I could do with it. Of course, the moment I began, I experienced the joy of translation, the excitement of making available in English a work that in one's opinion deserves wider attention, and the aggravation of being unable to find the right word, the right phrase and the right tone for what seems so exquisite, so effortless and so clear in the original poem.

Whatever its merits were as translation, and most likely it was a poor job, I showed that poem to my friends and they liked very much what they saw, which made me return to the library and continue to fill my notebook with contemporary Yugoslav poetry. Being an American poet of Serbian background made this entire endeavor much more than a literary exercise. I found myself between two cultural identities, two ways of looking at the world, and having to negotiate between them. To translate is to be aware not just of the differences between two languages and literary traditions, but equally of the way in which so much of what the native reader understands and appreciates in a poem is not to be found in the words on the page, but remains unspoken.

This is what drew me to it: the knowledge that what I was about to do might not be possible to accomplish. Many times over the years I had to give up on a poem because an image or a few lines could not be properly translated into English. In that respect, the predicament of the translator is no different from that of the poet, who often feels that he has not been able to find the exact word for a particular mood or experience, and had to settle for a rough equivalent. What the two of them have in common is an obsession with getting each bit of language right, and the belief that once in a while they can defy the gods, do the impossible and reach perfection.

Together with Novica Tadic, Radmila Lazic, Dusko Novakovic, Nina Zivancevic and one or two others, Milan Djordjević belongs to one of most remarkably talented generations of Serbian poets. He was born in 1954 in Belgrade in what was then Yugoslavia. His mother, who came from a wealthy family, became a communist before World War II out of a desire to abolish poverty and make society more just. This was a scandalous step for someone of her class and made her a black sheep in the family. After the German occupation and the end of a civil war in which she fought on the winning side, she became one of the directors of a prestigious publishing house. Nevertheless, in 1947 she was expelled from the Communist Party and eventually lost her job for supposedly allowing people in her office to criticize the leadership. His father was an architect and an anticommunist who worked in his youth in the British embassy, whose cultural attaché at that time was the novelist Lawrence Durrell, with whom he was friends. Milan Djordjević was thus a child of what the communist authorities in Yugoslavia at that time regarded as two enemies of the people. He grew up in Belgrade in a house his father built in the yard of the house belonging to his great-grandfather. Like all Balkan children, he learned about communism and anticommunism and what the great powers did to the small nations, listening to his parents talk.

As a young man, Djordjević wanted to go to art school and become a painter, but ended up studying world literature, since he loved books and had already begun writing poetry in high school after coming across some poems of Georg Trakl, the dark and visionary Austrian poet. His father often took him along on business trips both throughout Yugoslavia and abroad. Consequently, he lived for long stretches of time in Ljubljana, where he learned the language, began translating Slovenian poetry and prose into Serbian, and came under the influence of two leading postwar Slovenian poets, Dane Zajc and Tomaz Salamun. It was a milieu in which avant-garde arts and literature flourished within a small circle of men and women under the watchful and wary eye of the local Communist Party. Salamun, whose poetry incorporates such diverse influences as that of Walt Whitman, Velimir Khlebnikov and Frank O'Hara, was then the most innovative poet in Yugoslavia. Djordjević's first book of poems, *On Both Sides of the Skin,* which came out in 1979, is in no way as experimental and skilled as Salamun's poetry, but its occasional touches of surrealism and black humor recall the adventurous spirit of the older poet.

Djordjević's second book, *Fly and Other Poems,* which appeared in 1986, is a far more confident and successful collection. If the task of a young poet is to search for and discover an authentic voice and an original way of looking at things, these poems do that. They are short, often erotic, and startling in their imagery.

The Rain Wants to Kill Itself

With its fingers the rain stains your window and mumbles.
It wants to come in and kill itself.
I see you are in bed and couldn't care less.
In the dark. Naked. Couldn't care less.
Your hair loose. Your thighs spread open.
And there, in plain sight, black moss!
Your left middle finger busy, busy!
Villain, searching for the red crest.
While golden honey already oozes.
You call me from your delirium tremens.

Me already changed into a crow.

I fly down into your lap and peck, peck.

And then in my beak carry the caught fish away,

to go play cards and drink.

While the rain with its fingers

makes stains over your windowpanes and mumbles,

counts its beads,

wants to come in and kill itself.

In this and the other poems in the book a distinct persona begins to emerge, an obsessive, introspective and intense young man who, irrespective of whether he looks at an apple he is about to peel, or the dishes he's washing, encounters some surprising and troubling aspect of himself. "I speak of myself as of another, and of others as of myself," Djordjević has said. There's something else, too, present in these poems. Marxism is in disrepute nowadays, but its idea that political reality determines consciousness may have some relevance here. A dark cloud hangs over Djordjević's poems. He never spells out whether it is his own fate that worries him, or the world he lives in. Most likely, it is the combination of the two. Like his older contemporary, Novica Tadic, whom he most resembles in these early poems, Djordjević has a premonition of tragedy. Certainly, these "dark visions" of his are also a literary strategy, an attempt to disrupt the reader's expectations, strive for surprise, something never seen before, never heard before, as much as they are premonitions about the future. Still, reading these poems today, one can't help but recall the horrors that were soon to take place in Yugoslavia.

In books that followed, *Mummy, Amber and Garden* (both 1990) and *The Desert* (1995), Djordjević's poetry gradually begins to change. He's no longer interested in creating some new reality, but in examining the one that's already there. From a poet of surreal visions and wild imaginings, he becomes a poet of his own experience. Perhaps this new directness is to be attributed to the war taking place all around him and the prose he was writing in those years. In the 1990s, Djordjević was politically active as an opponent of the regime of Slobodan Milosevic, the rise of virulent nationalism, ethnic intolerance and violence. He wrote articles for opposition papers and participated in various dissident organizations and political parties. During this time he also wrote three collections of stories and one of essays. One cannot tell much about Djordjević's life from the earlier poems. Now, his life becomes his principal subject matter, and the voice we hear from poem to poem we begin to recognize as the voice of the man who writes these poems. Still, many of the techniques found in the earlier poems—compression, fragmentation, free association—as well as his love for the surprising image and detail, are still to be found in the poems of this period.

Orange

Like the cry of a seagull in the still air
above the empty beach where dark algae are drying,
The bluish blade cuts into her skin.

My fingers bare the nakedness of the orange lamp
so that with a scent of Crete it may light my room,
the way fresh water sprinkles a dry plant.

His next two books, *Clean Colors* (2002) and *Black Orange* (2004), distinguish themselves by their ambition and the high quality of the poems. Some, like "Aachen" and "Wilted City," are accounts of his wanderings around Europe. Their narrative flow is interrupted by many unanticipated transitions and asides, where past and present events alternate, and myth mingles freely with reality. The restless, solitary figure who is our guide in these poems is the poet himself, depicted as a kind of lost soul, a young man from another culture adrift in these forbidding and yet attractive foreign cities. As is true of many later poems of Djordjević, the recurring emotion is that of wonder. For him, as it had been for Chekhov, the simplest things are the most incredible ones.

What Emerson called "the common, the familiar, the near, the low, is worth spending one's life puzzling over."

Fire in the Garden (2007) and *Joy* (2008) received several important literary awards in Serbia, but that recognition of the high esteem with which his poetry was regarded was marred by personal tragedy. In January of 2007, Djordjević was hit by a car while crossing on the designated crosswalk one of the main streets in Belgrade. He was in a coma for several days and near death for weeks, but managed to pull through despite serious bodily injuries, and after months in the hospital, and an even longer period of rehabilitation to teach him to walk again, he came home an invalid. Since then he's been pretty much confined to his house and garden. Fortunately, he has used that time well, writing a lot of poetry and prose. In this book, I've included eleven poems from this period which are again different from his previous work. Even more direct and plain in their diction, they range from the ones like "Mr. Accident" and "Solitude" that refer to the accident that changed his life, to others that either recall the past or, as in this poem, take as their point of departure something that had occurred or that he had observed that day looking out of the window.

Two Pigeons

I watch them sitting on the electric wire
stretched black over our street.
It's a gloomy day, rainy, the sky is gray.
I see them pressed to each other.
The rain softly falls and wets their feathers.
They barely move their heads,
and never look at each other.
Is it love or warmth that keeps them close?
Are they shielding each other from cold raindrops?
I've no idea, I only note
the closeness of their bodies
on that black, thick wire,

two gray feathery beings
joined into a single question.
When next I happen to look outside,
I see the wire is empty,
as if they both suddenly took off flapping their wings,
god knows where or why.

I resisted placing Djordjević's poems in chronological order. It seemed to me that in a book of this length, it would not convey the unity of his work, the distinct sensibility that pervades all his poems, which I would call empathy, his need to place himself in the place of another, be it a drunken old Polish cook he bumps into while walking around London, or a spider spinning his web and catching flies on the wall of his room in Belgrade. Undoubtedly, his recent encounter with death has made what was always present in his poetry even more acute. The poet's mission is not to save the world, but to save some human experience from oblivion, these poems are saying. Not history or metaphysics, but mortality, not just his own, but that of every other creature, no matter how marginal, is the theme of many of these later poems. "The voice of poetry is the voice of one solitude addressing another solitude," Djordjević has written. The strange experience of watching a moment in time come and go, the compassion for all whose time may be up—hasn't that been one of the primary emotions in lyric poetry? Although his poems are written in free verse, they have a feel for form and economy of expression that recalls that tradition. They say what they have to say briefly, very simply, and very powerfully. I hope that these translations of mine convey some of their originality and their beauty.

Charles Simic
Strafford, NH, January 2010

PART I

2

Kaput leži. Na podu.
Bez kapi krvi u sebi.
Kaput leži. Umoran,
zgrčen, odbačen i crn.
—Kapute! Kapute! Kapute!
—Mili brate! Ustani! Ustani!
Barem klekni kraj tvog
Milana Djordjevića!
Mili brate zasipan
snegovima, kišama,
pogrdama, laskanjima,
čuvaru moje samoće!
Ustani! Ustani!
Tako ti praznih džepova,
ispuniću ih mojim šakama.
Prhnuće krilima u tebi.
Tako ti zjapećih rukava,
pustiću izmučene životinjice,
moje ruke, u tebi da gmižu!
I kaput poče da diše,
otvori oči, zadrhta,
pokrenu jedan rukav,
raširi krila, polete, zagrakta,
zaogrnu me svojim mrakom.
I sad sam njegova utroba.

Overcoat lies. On the floor.
Without a drop of blood in it.
Overcoat lies. Weary.   3
Crumpled, discarded and black.
—Overcoat! Overcoat! Overcoat!
—Dear brother! Rise! Rise!
At least kneel next to your
Milan Djordjević!
Dear brother, guardian of my solitude,
beaten with rain, snow,
curses, flatteries!
Rise! Rise!
I will feel your empty pockets
with my hands.
They'll flutter their wings in them.
Inside your gaping sleeves
I'll let the threadbare little animals
that are my arms crawl!
So it may begin to breathe
and open its eyes, shudder,
then move one sleeve,
spread its wings, fly, caw
and drape me with its darkness.
I, who am its blood and guts.

4

Kiša prstima po tvom prozoru mrlja,
mrmlja. Htela bi da uđe da se ubije.
A ja vidim. Ležiš u postelji. I baš te briga.
U mraku. Gola. Baš te briga.
Raspustila kosu. Raširila butine.
I gle, crne mahovine!
A prst srednjak leve ruke, radi li radi!
Zločinac, traži crvenu krestu.
I zlaćani med već pocurio.
I zoveš me iz svog delirijum tremensa.
A ja se u gavrana prometnuo.
Doletim u tvoje krilo i kljucam, kljucam.
A onda u kljunu odnesem uhvaćenu ribu,
pa odem da se kartam i pijem.
A kiša još uvek prstima
po tvom prozoru mrlja, mrmlja,
prebira amajlije,
htela bi da udje da se ubije.

With its fingers the rain stains your window and mumbles.
It wants to come in and kill itself.
I see you are in bed and couldn't care less.   5
In the dark. Naked. Couldn't care less.
Your hair loose. Your thighs spread open.
And there, in plain sight, black moss!
Your left middle finger busy, busy!
Villain, searching for the red crest.
While golden honey already oozes.
You call me from your delirium tremens.
Me already changed into a crow.
I fly down into your lap and peck, peck.
And then in my beak carry the caught fish away,
to go play cards and drink.
While the rain with its fingers
makes stains over your windowpanes and mumbles,
counts its beads,
wants to come in and kill itself.

6

Prvo ga je zavodila plavim očicama.

A on je zgrabio dlakavim ručerdama.

Kokoška se smejala, smejala.

Kao na kućnoj zabavi.

A on je nožićem zagolicao po vratu.

I nežno je položio na panj.

I odsekao.

I glava je pala sa osmehom na kljunu.

I telo je trčalo dvorištem

i za sobom vuklo rep,

crveni repić krvi

koja se razbaškarila po travi.

I dve vrane sedele na grani oraha.

Sedele i pušile. I rekle:

—Naraštaj jedan odlazi

i drugi dolazi,

a zemlja stoji u vijek!

—Sve je od praha

i sve se vraća u prah!

First, she seduced him with her blue eyes.
So he grabbed her with his hairy hands.
The hen laughed, laughed.
As if she were at a house party.
While he tickled her throat with a knife.
And gently laid her on the stump.
Cut her head off.
So it fell with a smile still in her beak.
And the body ran through the yard,
dragging the tail behind it,
the red tail of blood
settling down in the grass.
Two crows sat in a chestnut tree.
Sat smoking. And said:
One generation is on its way out,
another one is coming,
only the earth is forever.
—All is dust
and returns to dust!

Krompir |

U dubokoj grobnici ležao je,
blaženopočivši, faraon mrke boje.

Medju svojima žalostive suze je lio
za čestitim blatom u kome se ispilio.

Ali evo ga na tanjiru oholog, obarenog,
peršunom krunisanog, maslacem pomazanog,

evo ga samotnog, kao od majke rodjenog,
od gladi spasao je zatornika i pravednog.

Gle, vitki nož preseca ga napola,
gle, viljuška mu se u ledja zabola!

Ali, prijatelji, nemojte zato tugovati,
na svet krtola nemojte mračno gledati,

jer drugi spasitelji u vrećama klijaju,
da zvezdu-vodilju na vedrom nebu ugledaju.

In a deep tomb he lay,
a dark-hued pharaoh resting in peace.

In private, he shed grief-stricken tears
for the honest mud where he was hatched.

Here he is now on a plate, arrogant, boiled,
crowned with parsley, smeared with butter,

solitary like a newborn, he who saved
from hunger both the damned and the just.

Look, a thin knife cuts him in half.
Look, a fork sticks out of his back.

But, friend, don't feel sorry for them.
Don't look darkly on the world of potatoes,

since in sacks other saviors are sprouting
hoping to see the polestar some clear night.

10

O mali, beli korene oblih bokova,
kakvu krv piješ iz zemljine tmine?
Je li čaroban miris tvojih sokova?

Zemlja je tajna, mesto tmastih snova,
crnilo budjeno besom sunca i kišurine,
nežnošću snega i divljanjem vetrova.

O mali, beli korene oblih bokova,
hoćeš li sveopštu čorbu začiniti
ili ostati sred zemaljskih okova?

Tvoji mirisi spajaju lepotu beline
i ružnoću crnila, buku svih ratišta
i plavetno ništa okeanske tišine.

O mali i obli korene belih bokova,
teraš li Djavola svojim sokovima?
Jesi li moć kuhinje veselih bogova?

Ili si jestivo čudo što samo spaja
glupost i dubinu kao penis i vaginu
usred našeg elektronskoga Raja?

O small, white root with round hips,
what blood do you drink out of earth's darkness?
Is the scent of your sap magical?

The earth is secretive, the place of black dreams,
darkness wakened by the fury of sun and rain,
the tenderness of snow and savagery of winds.

O small, white root with round hips
will you flavor our communal soup
or will you remain in earth's chains?

Your scent brings together the beauty of whiteness,
the ugliness of black, the noise of battle
and the blue nothingness of oceanic silence.

O small, white root with round hips,
do you chase the devil away with your sap?
Do you rule the kitchen of carefree gods?

Or are you the edible miracle that couples
foolishness and depth, like penis and vagina,
in the midst of our electronic Paradise?

Naleće roj muva,
gomila ljudi.
Roj muva, gomila ljudi.

—Šta hoće od mene
koji sam samom sebi stranac?

—Pokaži ruke, pokaži?
Prao si prljave ruke?
U čiste ih pretvarao?

Pokazujem ruke moje savesti.
Pokazujem ruke ovce.
Pokazujem čistu krpu moje svesti.

—A sad kaži: Ovo je raj!
Ovo je raj!
Priznajem sud muvlje inkvizicije,
pravedne policije!

Upljuvan muhoserinama njihove mudrosti
kažem: —Ovo je raj! Ovo je raj!
A u sebi izgovaram:
—Neka idu u majčinu,
zemlja se ipak kreće!

I roj muva, gomila ljudi,
andjela čuvara,
pobednički odleće, odleće.

A swarm of flies attacks,
a crowd of men.
Swarm of flies, crowd of men.

—What do they want from me,
who even to myself am a stranger?

—Show your hands, show!
You washed your dirty hands?
Made them clean?

I show the hands to my conscience.
Show my sheep-like hands.
Show the clean rags of my mind.

Tell me now, this is heaven!
This is heaven! I accept the flies'
inquisition, their just police!

Spat all over with their shit-like wisdom.
I say this is heaven! Heaven!
The earth still turns
—and in a whisper, let them go to hell.

And the swarm of flies, crowd of men,
guardian angels,
triumphantly fly away, fly away.

San |

Kad dodjem do njegove oštre ivice,
do ivice na kojoj bih mogao da se posečem
kao što sam palac na ivici belog papira posekao,
kao što sam belo sečivo svojom krvlju obojio,
kada dodjem, pogledam dole i vidim drugi san
grozniji od ovoga, san u kojem me neko sanja
deset godina posle moje nagle i nasilne smrti.
Jer znam, svi moji snovi umreće onoga dana
kada me smrt odnese na mesto gde više neće biti
ni imena ulica, ni brojeva kuća, niti kakvih adresa.
Znam, svi moji dani biće kao trunje i fina prašina
ispod ovog seoskog kreveta na kojem sanjam.
Svi moji dani biće niz vedara punih mleka
ili niz kablica ispunjenih ponoćnim tečnostima
mračnijim i gušćim od istopljenoga katrana.
I sva će se vedra i kablice na kraju prosuti.
I tako svoje crnilo i belinu izmešati.

When I come to its sharp edge,
the sharp edge on which I may cut myself,
the way I cut my thumb on a sheet of white paper,   15
the way I colored its edge with my blood,
when I stood there, looked down, I saw a dream,
even more terrifying than this one,
a dream in which someone dreams of me
ten years after my sudden and violent death.
I know that all my dreams will die the day
death takes me to a place where streets
have no names, the houses no numbers or address.
I know all my days will be like crumbs and fine dust
under this country bed in which I lie dreaming.
My days will be a row of milk pails
and buckets filled with midnight liquids
darker and thicker than melted pitch,
so that in the end all the pails and buckets will be spilled
and everything dark and white in me will be mixed.

Veliko i malo | *za Aneliz Gotje*

Pesnik Bašo uči me kako slavna dela
vojskovodja, krvnika mogu postati ništa
a da skok žabe može trajati vekovima.

Sa Atlantika dolaze crni oblaci i kiša.
Bilo je sunčano a sad na Sen Nazer
kao pirinač sa neba padaju zrna leda.

Pesnici su bića često lišena suštine,
ljudi što govore gluposti i neistine,
lude i brbljivci koji svašta umišljaju.

Pa ipak, pa ipak, mrmljaju o čudima,
buncaju ono što drugi ne naslućuju,
a reči u mraku fosforno im blistaju.

Japanski pesnik Bašo uči me
da blisko može biti užasno daleko
a put u daljinu približavanje sebi.

Iznad Atlantika smračilo se nebo
i pljuštao je sitan led a sada grad
ozaruju bleštanje sunca i vedrina.

Great and Small | *for Anne-Lise Gautier*

The poet Basho teaches that the famous feats
of blood-soaked military leaders come to nothing
while a leap of a frog may last centuries.

Black clouds and rain arrive from the Atlantic.
The sun was out, but now over Saint-Nazaire
The grains of ice fall out of the sky like black rice.

Poets are creatures often lacking in substance,
men who say stupid and untrue things,
madmen and blabbermouths who imagine what they will.

And yet, and yet, they whisper about miracles,
rant about what others don't even suspect,
so their words glow in the dark like phosphorus.

The Japanese poet Basho teaches me
that what is close may be terrifyingly distant and that a journey
to a far-off place brings one closer to oneself.

Over the Atlantic, the sky has darkened,
hail fell just a moment ago, and now the city glistens
in the sunshine and under the clear sky.

Dosad sam samo zamišljao plovidbu,
a sad ću se stvarno ukrcati na brod,
sad ću jednostavno isploviti iz luke.

Izložiću se fijukanju ledenih vetrova,
golemim talasima i čudima Atlantika.
Oslobodiću se maštarija i sanjarenja.

Napustiću sve jednolično i beskrvno.
Odbaciću svu jalovost zamišljanja.
Disaću kao životinja, biću mornar.

Počeću zaista vešto da skačem i petljam
oko brodske snasti i čvorova konopaca.
I rasplićem sve što je davno zamršeno.

Evo me, iskusni mudri morski vukovi,
siroče sam, na kopnu nikom potrebno.
Neka me zato usvoji ustalasani okean.

Primite me, kapetani najduže plovidbe,
menjam suvu dosadu zemaljske izvesnosti
za beskraj uzbudljive neizvesnosti vode.

Primite me, vi što klizite plavetnilom,
vi koji ste sve dalje od prve nevine luke,
primite me da pobedim strah i da se nadam.

Up to now I only imagined a sea voyage,
and now I'm about to embark on a ship,
now I'm about to sail out of the harbor.

I'll expose myself to the howling of cold winds,
the huge waves and moods of the Atlantic.
I'll free myself from daydreams and imaginings.

I'll leave behind everything drab and bloodless.
I'll reject all idle thoughts.
I'll breathe like an animal; I'll be a sailor.

I'll begin truly to busy myself with ship's
riggings and knotted ropes, untangling
what had been tangled long ago.

Here I am, wise and experienced sea wolves,
I'm an orphan, no one needs me on land.
Let the choppy ocean adopt me as its own.

Take me, captain, you of the longest voyage,
I'm exchanging the dry boredom of land's certainties
for the thrill and infinite uncertainty of the sea.

Take me, you who glide over the blue,
you, farther than ever from the first innocent harbor,
take me along so I can conquer my fear and hope.

20

Tražim stazu ili pravi put izmedju poljana
zasoljenih injem i sitnim snegom, zarobljenih
bodljikavim žicama, tražim sigurnu stazu
ili smrznuti put koji će me odavde odvesti.
Tražim stazu kojom ću mirno da koračam.
Vidim jastreba, sa usamljenog hrasta uzleće,
pa širi krila i spušta se ka ogoleloj šumi.
Vidim dve vrane gde na drugoj strani kruže.
Jutros je zec munjevito protrčao kroz baštu.
Ovce se kraj ograde skupljaju i tupo zure.
U daljini, iznad šume helikopter nisko leti.
Nisam potpuno siguran u ono što vidim.
Nisam potpuno siguran u ono što čujem.
Krv mi kroz umorno telo jednolično struji.
Mislim na crvenu grčku pomorandžu.
Iz njenog mesa sunčeva slast brzo se cedi.
Mislim na oblinu jedne dojke koju u tami
pre mnogo godina nisam na rastanku poljubio.
Tražim dobru stazu ili put izmedju poljana.
Ponavljam staru, naučenu lekciju o traženju.
Njušim vazduh i s brda gledam naseljenu dolinu.
Žalostan sam kao zardjala šerpa u jarku.
Žalostan sam kao kondenzovano mleko u frižideru.
Noću zijam u psihodeličnu belinu meseca.
Melanholičan sam kao pogrešno ispisani formular.
Ali posle tumaranja našao sam pouzdanu stazu,
našao sam put koji vodi do središta maloga grada.
Tu ću popiti pivo i odatle ću ti, daleki prijatelju,
odatle ću, kao da snežnu grudvu niz brdo kotrljam,
odatle ću ti poslati ovu nešifrovanu elegičnu poruku.

I seek a path or a road between the fields,
salted with black frost and fine snow, imprisoned
by barbed wire, I seek a reliable path   21
or a frozen road that will take me from here.
I seek a path I can walk on calmly.
I see a hawk take flight from a lone oak tree,
spread its wings and dive toward the leafless forest.
I see two crows circling on the other side.
This morning a rabbit dashed through the garden.
Now the sheep gather at the fence and stare dumbly.
In the distance a helicopter flies over the forest.
I'm not entirely sure what I'm seeing.
I'm not entirely sure what I'm hearing.
The blood flows evenly through my tired body.
I'm thinking about a red orange from Greece.
The way sweet sunlight drips from her pulp.
I'm thinking about a round breast in the dark
which saying goodbye years ago I didn't kiss.
I seek a solid path or a road between the fields.
I repeat all the well-learned lessons about being lost.
I sniff the air and gaze from a hill at the populated valley.
I'm as sad as a rusty cooking pot thrown in a ditch,
as sad as the condensed milk in the refrigerator.
At night I stare at the psychedelic whiteness of the moon
as sad as the wrongly filled-out official form.
After much roaming around, I found a dependable path,
I found a road that leads into the center of a small town.
There I will have a beer, and will send you, distant friend,
with the speed of a snowball rolling down a hill,
this elegiac message free of covert meanings.

Hleb |

Tako spokojno leži
na dasci za sečenje.
Ima oblik dobrote.

Blaženo nam tako leži.
Čeka kratku presudu,
nož u ledja, komadanje.

U hlebu je ceo svet.
Ali samo ga zagrizi
kao telo Božjeg sina.

Samo ga zagrizi.
Prelomi mu koru.
I nastaće tišina.

Tišina s početka,
ah, blistava tišina
na kraju sveta.

It has the shape of goodness.
How peacefully it lies
on the cutting board.

Blissfully awaiting the quick verdict,
the knife in the back
or being torn into chunks.

The whole world is a loaf of bread.
Bite into it
as if it were the body of God's only son.

Go ahead and do it,
break the crust
and the silence will fall.

The silence of the beginning,
Ah, the blazing silence
as the world ends.

Sneg pada na smrznutu zemlju. Sneg pada.
U tišini kao da čujem šum njegovog padanja,
šuštanje tkanine ili pucketanje plamena.

U tišini gustoj kao milijarde čestica
rasprskavanja Nijagarinog vodopada
ili obrušavanja usova na Himalijima.

Sneg se roji i na fotografiji iz Japana.
A na njoj bonze u narandžastim odorama,
pod kišobranima od trske, uhvaćeni.

Uhvaćeni dok idu kraj zida vrta, kraj hrama
i crnih borova, zauvek na slici zaustavljeni
u tišini zgrušanoj padanjem suvog snega.

Ova tišina je večnost i neponovljivo.
Ona je nežnost i mekoća ptičjeg paperja
i milina oktobarskog popodneva boje meda.

Ona je prašina sa drvenih polica za knjige
ili samo žudnja starca za bezbrižnošću
i beskrajnom slašću detinjstva, Pardesa,
svežeg poput ukusa tek ubrane jagode.

The snow falls on the frozen earth. The snow falls.
In the silence I think I hear the sound of its fall,
like the rustle of a cloth, or the crackling of a fire.

In the silence as thick as billions of particles
of an exploding Niagara,
or the slide of some Himalayan avalanche.

In a photograph from Japan, swarming with snow,
there are monks in orange robes
under umbrellas made of bamboo.

They were caught walking past a garden wall
and some black pine trees arrested forever
in a silence solidified by the falling snow.

This silence is eternal and never to be repeated.
She has the gentleness and softness of bird feathers,
the bliss of October afternoon the color of honey.

She's the dust from wooden bookshelves,
the yearning of an old man for the freedom
and the endless sweetness of childhood. Paradise,
as fresh as the taste of just-picked strawberries.

26

Da, i ti ćeš mi konačno doći,
mala, obična, dnevna radosti.
Bićeš komad ražanog hleba
ili čaša puna ledenog mleka.

I dok tmasti oblaci klize nebom
i pomalja se njuška dragog sunca,
osetiću te čak na jeziku i nepcima.
I postaćeš mi devojka lepih dojki.

O mala, crvena, praznična radosti,
poljubiću ti svaki delić nagog tela,
odneću te u postelju i milovati.
I usnuću kao zemlja pored vrela.

Yes, you, too, will finally come.
A small, ordinary, daily joy.
You'll be the slice of rye bread,   27
or a glass filled with cold milk.

And while the dark clouds fly in the sky,
and the beloved sun pokes its nose, I'll feel you
even on my tongue and my palate,
so you become to me a girl with beautiful breasts.

O little, red, festive joy,
I'll kiss every part of your naked body,
Carry you to bed, caress you,
and sleep the way the earth sleeps next to a spring.

28

Jedne letnje večeri dečak stoji na pločniku,
stoji pred akvarijumom u izlogu restorana.
Iz obasjanog akvarijuma motre ga tamne oči
pastrmki, karaša ili možda tustih šarana.
Kraj njega je ćutljivi otac i drži ga za ruku.
Ribe miruju medju mehurićima u zelenoj vodi.
U ribljim očima dečak možda vidi strah.
Za ribe možda je spasitelj iz obližnje ulice,
možda njihova poslednja nada i ozarenje.
Riblje oči i usta iza stakla kao da mu govore:
"Spasi nas, dečače! Oslobodi nas, oslobodi!
Zdrobi zid našeg providnog i uskog kaveza!"
Dečak gleda riblja usta i oči, pa sporo prilazi
i kamenom razbija staklo zelenog akvarijuma.
I ustreptale ribe sa vodom padaju na crni asfalt.
I srebrno se praćakaju medju staklićima.
I kao dečakova šaka krvare i dišu slobodne.
Krvare, panično otvaraju usta i sluzave škrge.
I, spasene, udišu mlaku noć, dišu i sahnu.
A tama i blede boje grada razlivaju im se
po blistavim krljuštima i ranjenim bokovima.

One summer night a boy stands on the sidewalk
before an aquarium in the window of a restaurant.
Dark eyes of trout, carps, small and fat,
watch him from the lit up aquarium.
Next to him his quiet father holds him by the hand.
The fish are still in the green water among rising bubbles.
In their eyes perhaps the little boy sees fear.
For them, he's the savior from the next street,
perhaps, their last hope and joy.
Behind the glass, their eyes and mouths tell him:
"Save us, boy! Free us all, free us!
Break the walls of our narrow, transparent cage!"
The boy watches their eyes and mouths, slowly approaches
and with a rock breaks the green aquarium.
The flapping fish spill on the black asphalt,
wiggling, all-silvery, amidst the broken glass,
and bleed like the boy's hand while breathing freely.
Bleed, their mouths and slimy gills open in panic.
Rescued, they gasp for air in the mild night and die.
While darkness and pale colors of the city
flow over their glittering scales and wounded sides.

30

Kažem ti, prijatelju, varvari dolaze
da osveže krv planinskih reka, da toljagama
premlate umorne kipove i podviknu: Marš u istoriju!
Varvari imaju sunce u očima i džepove pune praziluka.
Sriču dok čitaju, a posle izriču stroge estetske sudove.
Još uvek su zeleni i sentimentalni. Mrko gledaju
na vidre i lavove. Brkati varvari oslobadjaju
od pamuka. Sa živih leševa i orhideja skidaju
šminku i puder. Šamaraju narodne neprijatelje,
vampire, a onda balerinama prave talentovanu decu,
buduće sataniste.

I'm telling you friend, barbarians are coming
to refresh the blood of mountain brooks,
with clubs to work over the weary statues and shout:
Run along into History! The barbarians
have sun in their eyes and pockets full of leek.
They mumble to themselves while they read and then
immediately make severe aesthetic judgments.
They are wet behind the ears and sentimental.
They look with suspicion on otters and lions.
Mustachioed barbarians are liberating us from cotton.
From living corpses and orchids
they'll wipe off makeup and powder.
They slap the enemies of the people, vampires,
and then with ballet dancers
make talented children, future Satanists.

PART II

34

Neka je hvaljena lepotica lažno plave kose
i neka joj se, Gospode, jednom u nebo vaznesu
guzovi snimljeni kamerama, nevini poput rose,
praćeni sisama u koje su upumpali silikone,
što se tresu ili joj se bele kao noge bose.
Neka se zemlja, voda, vazduh i vatra poklone
obrijanoj mindži i ćubi sa Čiroki frizurom.
Toliko uloga, Gospode, i stenjanja i cičanja
u kolor filmovima za odrasle i nevaljalu decu.
Toliko krupnih planova, toliko donjih rakursa.
Raj je ovaploćen u velikom studiju porno industrije.
Raj je film gde umetnici vežbaju Figurae Veneris,
gde vibratori nežno zuje a glumice nemaju strije.
Tolike devičanske postelje u koje se hitro ulazi
i toliko suvišne odeće iz koje se još brže izlazi.
Neka je hvaljena božanstvena blondinka Džena,
gologuzanka što se stvarno profesionalno mazi
i prodaje vrhunsku robu iz seksualne oblasti.
Neka je hvaljena mlečnobela kao morska pena.
Koliko uspešnog glumljenja zanosa i strasti,
ljubavi, drhtanja i vrhunca slatkog orgazma
i sličnih nezemaljskih i natprirodnih pojava
što su kao kakva divna i spasonosna spazma
između plazme sna i onoga što je okrutna java.
A vi što je osudjujete u ime Boga, čiste metafizike,
porodičnog morala i sličnih fantomskih isparenja,

Let the beauty with faux blonde hair be praised,
and let, oh Lord, her ass, innocent as dew
caught on numerous cameras, ascend to heaven
followed by her teats pumped full with silicon,
that shake, or are as white as bare feet.
Let the earth, water, air and fire bow down
to her shaved pussy and her Mohawk hairdo.
So many roles, Lord, moaning and screaming
in color films for adults and naughty children.
So many big plans, so many overhead camera views.
That heaven has been incarnated in great movie studios
        of porno industry.
That heaven is a film where actors rehearse coital positions,
where vibrators softly hum and actresses have no cellulite lines.
So many virginal beds into which one jumps quickly,
And so many extra clothes one is in even bigger hurry to shed.
Let the divine blonde Jenna be praised,
the bare-assed one who know how to cuddle like a pro,
and peddle top sexual merchandise.
Let her milky whiteness be celebrated like sea foam.
How many well-acted scenes of ecstasy and passion,
love, palpitation and peaks of sweet orgasm,
and similar unearthly and supernatural occurrences
which are like a glorious and beatific link
between the plasma of dreams and cruel reality.
As for you who condemn in the name of God pure metaphysics,
family values and similar phantom vapors,

sada pojačajte ton i slušajte njene radosne krike,
i, molić u lepo, dragi moji, tu se nema šta kriti,
pre gledanja filmova o umetnosti parenja
shvatite, njeno telo je poput nebeske muzike
iz koje se zdušno izvlače zemaljski profiti.

36

turn the volume higher and hear her joyous screams,
and, I beg you kindly, my dears, there's nothing to hide,
before watching films about the art of coupling,
please understand, her body is like heavenly music,
from which ardent earthly profits are derived.

38

Nedeljom popodne Ahen je prazan kao džep moga kaputa.
Po ulicama grada trupkaju samo znatiželjni i umorni turisti,
Japanci, Poljaci, Amerikanci, možda Arapi ili Belgijanci.
Toplo je u ahenskoj katedrali kao u vunenoj rukavici.
Posle telefoniranja, automat mi guta plastičnu karticu,
pa pišti i ne želi da je iz svojih metalnih usta vrati.
O, svojeglavi automate božanstva, svetog Telekoma,
zašto gutaš ono što je moje, zašto me onemogućavaš
da čujem sve one koji su mi bliski, prijatni ili dragi?
Zašto me sprečavaš da tim komadićem plastike
spajam prošlost i budućnost, sever i jug, inje i toplinu,
gladne ptice i site insekte, fantazije i golu stvarnost?
Zašto izazivaš moj bes i gnev balkanskog pravednika?
Želiš li da te udarcem pesnice odmah podsetim
da zaista praviš tešku i neoprostivu istorijsku grešku?
Ulice Ahena prazne su ovog nedeljnog popodneva,
prazne su kao osušeno pčelinje saće u košnici.
Ne znam kakve me sve tajanstvene sile gone
da u Ahenu po mrazu tumaram kao da je leto.
Prijatelja nisam susreo u ahenskoj katedrali.
Na kamenom tlu okolnih ulica sede prosjaci.
Možda sam i ja samo prosjak koji bi da umilostivi
sve raznolike sile vode, vatre, zemlje i vazduha.
Možda sam prosjak koji na sumornom severu traži
samo ono što će dobiti od jarkih boja i crvenice juga.
I napuštam Ahen sa narandžastom kartom u džepu.
Ostavljam Ahen i zahvaljujem se moćnom božanstvu

Aachen |

On a Sunday afternoon, Aachen is as empty as the pocket of my coat.
Only curious and tired tourists trudge its streets,
Japanese, Polish, Americans, perhaps Arabs or Belgians. 39
It's warm in the Aachen cathedral as in a woolen glove.
After making a call, the public telephone eats my plastic card,
hisses and won't give it back from its metal mouth.
O, stubborn automatic deity of the saintly Telekom,
why do you swallow what is mine, why do you prevent me
from hearing those who are close, dear and agreeable to me?
Why do you thwart me from connecting the past and the future,
north and south, frost and heat, hungry birds and sated insects,
fantasy and naked reality, with this piece of plastic?
Why do you provoke the rage and fury of this righteous man
        from the Balkans?
Do you want me to remind you right now with my fist
that you are making a bad and unforgivable historical mistake?
The streets of Aachen are empty this Sunday afternoon,
empty like dried out honeycomb in a beehive.
I don't know what mysterious forces are making me
roam frosty Aachen as if it were summer.
I didn't meet my friend in the Aachen cathedral.
On the stone sidewalks of the surrounding streets beggars sit.
Perhaps I'm only a beggar trying to induce pity
in all the mighty forces of water, fire, earth and air.
Perhaps I'm only a beggar seeking in the gloomy north
what he can only get from the bright colors and red earth of the south.
I'm leaving Aachen with orange ticket in my hand.
I'm leaving Aachen saying thanks to the mighty deity

telekomunikacije, nemačkom Telekomu i njegovom slugi,
metalnom automatu što mi je vratio telefonsku karticu.
Pomoću nje uspostaviću veze među stvorenjima prošlosti
i budućnosti, izmedju svih bliskih i dalekih stvari,
jesenjeg cinobera, vatrinog žara i zimskog leda.

of telecommunication, German Telekom, and its servant
the metal automat which gave me back my telephone card.
With her help I'll reestablish ties between creatures
of the past and future, all distant and near things,
autumn's colors of cinnabar, embers from a fire and winter ice.

42

Probuditi se posle košmarne noći
ozaren mirisima i jasnom svetlošću.
Svež ustati iz postelje, pa izreći
prve reči, da budu inje. S blagošću
i tepanjem, detinje ih izgovarati
i kao sanik milovati usnula bića.
Gladan se radovati jednostavnosti.
Udisati crno kafe i prhkost peciva.
Iza zverske vreve, iza ljudske taštine
otkrivati reči kao u šumi kupine.
I, recimo, stariti kako dan stari,
kako biljni epiderm u avgustu zri
ili možda u mraku buradi merlo vri
i u jutru naći ono što nikad ne kopni.

1990–1993

He woke after a nightmarish night,
his face lit up with clear light and scents.
To rise refreshed out of bed, pronounce
the first, hoary words, say them
with tenderness, babbling as a child would,
and like the early snow caress the ones still sleeping.
To be hungry and to rejoice, how simple that is.
Inhale black coffee and the crispness of rolls.
Beyond the beastly din, beyond human vanity,
find words the way one finds blackberries in the woods.
And, hopefully, grow old as the day grows old,
as the plant seeds ripen in August,
or the wine in the darkness of a barrel,
and in this hour find what is deathless.

1990–1993

44

I oblaci imaju svoju istoriju.
Istoriju nastajanja, trajanja
i postepenog iščezavanja.

Ljudska istorija je priča
o prolivanju krvi i zločinu.
Istorija oblaka je nežnija.

Istorija oblaka je bela.
Oblaci se zgušnjavaju
pod raznim imenima.

Vedrinom klize nalik ribama,
snežnim grudvama, dojkama
ili drugim ženskim oblinama.

Podsećaju na san o večnosti,
na ono što u ljubavnim igrama
stvaraju nebo, voda i zemlja.

Oblaci su zgrušavanje mleka,
pretvaranje kapi u guste rojeve,
nagomilavanje gvalja pamuka.

Njihova istorija je nežna
i paperjasta i olujno tamna,
ispisivana ratovima munja.

Oblaci pripadaju istoriji neba
i uzvišenih nebeskih zbivanja
a ne istoriji kruženja vode.

Clouds too have their history.
History of coming into being,
thriving and gradually vanishing.

Human history is a story
of spilled blood and crime.
The history of clouds is more tender.

Clouds change shape
bearing different names.
The history of clouds is white.

In the clear sky they glide resembling fish,
snowballs, breasts,
and other female shapes.

They recall the dream of eternity,
what the sky, the earth and the water
made out of their love games.

Clouds are the curdling of milk,
the transformation of drops into swarms,
the accretion of cotton balls.

Their history is tender,
and feathery and dark as a storm
written by lightning at war.

They belong to the sky's history,
the lofty heavenly happenings
and the history of water.

Davno su bogovi odavde otišli
i sve ostavili na milost i nemilost
ništavilu istorije i konačnosti.

Davno su bogovi odavde izvetrili
samo su na vedrom nebu zaboravili
oblake, oblake što kao i mi prolaze.

Oblake što imaju burnu istoriju.
Istoriju nastajanja, belog trajanja
i postepenog i naglog iščezavanja.

Long ago the gods left us,
leaving everything at the mercy
of history and our mortality.

Long ago the gods decamped,
forgetting only the clouds in the clear sky,
clouds, clouds, that pass away like us.

Clouds have their stormy history.
History of coming into being, thriving,
and slow or sudden disappearance.

Tražiš odgovore na svoja pitanja, jer ne znaš ko si,
odakle dolaziš i kuda ideš? Tražiš tačne odgovore
u snovima iz Starog zaveta, u nejasnim sećanjima.

Ali, možda su odgovori u gutljajima crnog vina
čiji te opori ukus vodi do grozda ili crvenice
sredozemnog ostrva ili do dunavskih zelenih obala.

Možda su odgovori u opojnosti udahnutog dima
avganistanskog hašiša ili u beličastim kućama
u primorju Tunisa, možda u vlažnoj utrobi dagnje?

Ili u ječanju žene, u svim groznicama i slastima?
Ali to nisu odgovori, to nisu nikakvi odgovori.
Odgovori su ono što ćeš učiniti, slepi čoveče!

Oni su možda u posecanju stabla u beogradskoj bašti,
u gnječenju ploda višnje što ti prste boji tamnocrveno?
Ili su u tebi, jer u idućem ratu usmrtićeš prijatelja.

A možda ćeš jedne noći, posle dugotrajne olujine,
u samotnoj kući kraj razjarenog Atlantika otkriti
da je svet priča koju je izgovorio neko zaboravan.

Neko ko priču nikada ne ponavlja, neko ko baš nikada,
nikada neće doći, mada ga prizivaju, mada ga uvek čekaju,
kao što spržena Gobi čeka da topla kiša na nju pada.

You seek answers to your questions, since you don't know
    who you are,
where you come from and where you are going? You seek
    exact answers
in dreams, from the Old Testament, in vague memories.

Perhaps the answers are in sips of red wine
whose tart taste leads to the mold and the grape
of a Mediterranean island or the Danube's green banks?

Perhaps the answer lies in the intoxication of swallowed smoke
of hashish from Afghanistan, the white houses
in the seaside Tunis, in the wet entrails of a mussel?

Or the sobbing of a woman, in fever and in pleasure?
But those are not the answers, those are not real answers.
Blind man, the answers are to be found in things you will do!

They are perhaps in the sawn off tree in a garden in Belgrade,
in the juice of a sour cherry that colors your fingers dark red?
Or they are inside you, since in the next war you'll kill a friend.

And it may be that one night after a lengthy storm
in a solitary house next to the wild Atlantic, you'll discover
that the world is a story told by someone forgetful.

Someone who never repeats the story, someone who will never,
never come, though they call him, though they wait for him,
the way the parched Gobi Desert waits for hot rain.

50

Stojim na praznom pločniku, pred izlozima.
Kao nagotu grad mi pokazuje svoju tamnu stranu.
Grimiznocrvene odsjaje uhvaćene u prozorima,
sve ono što je nalik na tvoju i moju živu ranu.

Jesen je, doba žutomrkog lišća kestena, topola,
klenova, vreme jare zalazaka i hladjenja reka.
Septembarska svetlost gasne, a iz dubine Dorćola
niče ljubičasta senka, širi se gola ispolinka.

Teče tama niz plavičaste ulice, put mirnog Dunava,
sliva se niz Terazije, klizi po suvim travnjacima,
guta Kalemegdan, Ružicu i ogolelost Ratnog ostrva,
pohodi zapuštene bašte Senjaka, gusne u parkovima.

Sad prekriva krošnje Topčidera, gušte Košutnjaka
i tad odlazim, vraćam se tamo gde ću ledenom vodom
pokvasiti lice i onda nad sobom čuti poklič osvetnika,
pa u najgušćoj tami otkriti grozno obličje andjela,
obličje našeg zatornika, i dalje nasmejanog Samaela.

I stand on the empty sidewalk, before shop windows.
The city shows me its dark side in its nakedness.
Purple-red reflections caught in the windows,
everything like your open wound and mine.

It's autumn, the season of dark yellow chestnut leaves,
poplars, maples, the season of fiery sunsets and cooling rivers.
September light dies, and from the depth of Dorćol,
violet shadow grows and spreads like a naked giantess.

Darkness flows down a blue street toward the calm Danube,
pours into the main square, slides over the dry lawns,
swallows Kalemegdan, Ruzica and the bare War Island,
visits the unkempt gardens in Senjak, thickens in parks,

covers the trees of Topčider, the bushes of Košutnjak,
and so I go there where I can sprinkle my face
with cold water and then above hear the cry of the avenger,
and in thickest darkness discover the monstrous shape
     of the angel,
the shape of our doom, the still smiling Samael.

Igra | *Draganu Velikiću*

Smejao se, jer mogao je da bude sve i ništa.
Igrao se, kamenjem gadjao ulične sijalice,
cepao teniske patike na betonu igrališta,
ranjavao kolena, od kuće bežao put reke,
stajao na rubu provalije, ulazio u pećinu.
Iz kaveza dečaštva potom je naglo izašao
i opet se igrao: putovao je, pio recinu
na plaži u Solunu, slasti leta okusio,
u sobi drhtao nad obnaženom Ruskinjom.
A sada se igra bez reči, smeha ili gneva.
Zgrožen ljudskom glupošću i svirepošću,
žudi za zrelošću oktobarskih popodneva,
sa ledenim savršenstvom dijamanta i tišine
na kraju ovog umornog veka—odurne jazbine.

1990–1993

The Game | *for Dragan Velikic*

He laughed because he was able to be everything and nothing.
He played, threw rocks at street lights,
wore out his sneakers on the concrete playground,
scraped his knees, ran away from home along the river,
stood at the edge of a cliff, entered a cave.
From the cage of his childhood he walked out suddenly
and again played: traveled, drank retsina
on the beach in Salonika, tasted the pleasures of summer,
stood trembling in a room over an unclothed Russian girl.
Now he plays without words, without laughter or anger,
shocked by human stupidity and cruelty.
He yearns for the ripeness of October afternoons
with their diamond-like icy and silent perfection
at the conclusion of this tired century—our loathsome lair.

1990–1993

U kaljevu peć ispunjenu crvenkastim žarom od čamovih cepanica
ubacio sam omekšalu mandarinu što već beše počela da se kvari.
Njena kora i meso zacvrčali su kao krvavi komad junetine na vatri.

Iz te još sočne mandarine suknula je bela para, kora je pucala,
iz ploda je navirao vreli sok ali narandžasti plod pocrneo je začas,
pretvorio se u crno jaje i ostao šćućuren u gnezdu od žeravice.

Tako i mi, ubačeni u ovaj svet kao u golemu peć, brzo gorimo
da sagorimo, ugljenišemo se, postanemo pepeo koji treba razvejati
jer tako zapoveda Ništa u koje će svi živi ljudi jednoga dana verovati.

In a stove filled with reddish, fir-wood embers
I threw a tangerine that had gone soft and rotten.
Its skin and flesh sizzled like a chunk of beef in the fire.   55

White steam rose out of the juicy tangerine, its skin burst,
hot liquid bubbled up, but the fruit darkened instantly,
turned into a black egg snuggled in a nest of flying sparks.

Just so we are thrown into life as on a stove and quickly set ablaze,
to burn down, to become charred and turn into ashes that
        need to be dispersed as Nothing commands
in whom, one day, all the living creatures will come to believe in.

56

Od čega se ona sastoji ili od čega je sastavljena?
Od kamičaka, reči, kretnji, od talasa, mrazeva,
seksa, mirisa ili od slika, bledih i žestokih slika?
Od umiranja, boleština, ljubavi i još od milijardu
drugih važnih, manje važnih ili nevažnih stvari
i bića koja nam se poput nekog vrlo glasnog krika
približavaju, udaljavaju, približavaju, udaljavaju?
Ili tek od jednog ogromnog i ispolinskoga daha
koji sve prožima ali jako ga je teško primetiti?
A mi ga samo naslućujemo, možda ga udišemo,
i pratimo noć i dan, kišu, vetar, sneg, sjaj sunca
i gotovo svaki strašni ili tek mirni san, san, san.
Kao kapljanje pomorandžinog soka i letenje
crvenih latica sveže a upravo otkinute bulke.
A okružuje nas stvarnost, to veliko obilje.
Plitka kao bara, kao živi vulkan duboka.
U samom oku ali i ispod znatiželjnog oka.
Teče i menja se kao oblost u čistu ravninu
i plameni urlik u podvodnu najdublju tišinu.
Stvarnost voćnog ploda, mesa i zemljinog soka.
Stvarnost metala, betona i suvih i golih utrina,
beli fosfor, neshvatljiv kao oštra brazgotina
na hrastu ili sok što kaplje iz voćnih oblina,
stvarnost kamena, vode ili peščanih dina.

Of what does it consist, of what is it made?
From pebbles, words, motion, waves, winter freeze,
sex, scents, or from images, pale and powerful images?
Of death, illness, love and a million other
important, less important, or unimportant things
and beings which like a loud scream come closer,
grow more distant, come closer, grow more distant?
Or, perhaps, from one huge breath
that penetrates everything though it's hard to see?
We only have an inkling of it, perhaps we breathe it
while keeping tabs on night and day, the rain, the wind,
     the snow, the light of the sun,
and nearly every terrifying or pleasant dream, dream, dream.
Like the drip of orange juice and the flight
of petals from the freshly picked poppy.
Reality surrounds us with its great wealth.
Shallow as a puddle, deep as an active volcano.
In the very eye, or in the squint of someone curious,
it flows and changes like a hill into the flat country
and a fiery howl in the underwater silence.
The reality of a fruit, meat and earth's dampness.
The reality of metal, concrete, dry and naked meadows,
white phosphorus, incomprehensible like a sharp cut
on an oak tree, or the juice that oozes out of a round fruit,
the reality of stone, water and sand dunes.

Bila su dva veća pauka.
Došli su iz vlage dvorišta.
I šetali su po belom zidu.
Baš kao da im nije ništa.
Žena ih je brzo pojurila.
Jednog je udarcem usmrtila.
Drugi se sakrio iza knjiga.
Knjige poezije su ga spasle.
Izgleda, sada je bez briga.
Na zidu se opet baškari.
Plete svoju mrežu i lovi:
mušice, bubice, sitna bića.
Njima se gospodin hrani.
Gledam, insekti su življi
od mene usred svetlosti
i tople ili hladnije tmine.
Insekti, veći ili oni manji,
majušnog života šamani.

There were two large spiders.
They came from the damp yard,
and walked over the white wall
as if they had no care in the world.
The wife quickly chased them.
Killed one with a single slap.
The other hid behind the books.
Poetry books saved him.
Now it seems he has no worry.
He takes it easy on the wall.
Weaves his web and hunts
gnats, bugs, minute beings.
That's how Mister feeds himself.
I see in the light that his insects
amid the warmer and cooler shadows
look more alive than I am.
Insects, bigger or smaller,
shamans of their tiny little life.

"Sve putem koji vodi slavi
  krenuše kao vojske mraka,"
  kaže pesnik ali sada se sećam:
  moj greh prema njima još je veći.
  I oni su mi, mrki i crni, naseljavali
  detinjstvo, nadgledao sam ih s visine
  i štapićem čeprkao po mravinjacima
  i sipao vodu "u noći tudjeg mravinjaka."
  Ili sam im spaljivao uspaničena telašca
  lupom usmerivši na njih zrak sunca.
  Sećam se i slatkog mirisa te paljevine.
  I skvrčenih mrava, sada bića tmine.
"Svud ostavivši smrt i senke."
  I kao da osećam svetu vlažnost
  i nimalo laki miris neke ženke.

"On the road that leads to glory,
  they set out like an army of darkness,"
  the poet wrote, and now my sin toward them
  seemed even greater.
  Brown and black, they colonized my childhood.
  I watched them from high above
  and with a stick poked and poured water
"in the night of a strange anthill."
  Or I set them on fire aiming a magnifying glass
  at their panicked bodies
  I even remember the sweet smell of that fire,
"everywhere leaving death and shadows,"
  and the contorted ants, now beings of darkness,
  feeling something holy and moist,
  the nearly unbearable smell of female sex.

Usvojio nas je mačak Darvin,
taj debeljuca i pametni lutalica.
Izabrao je da kod nas boravi.
Ponekad u ovoj kući prespava.
A više puta na dan ga hranim.
Žao mi je tog uličnog mačka.
A već sam ga prilično zavoleo.
Glava i uši su mu puni ožiljaka.
Biće da zelenooki ne vidi dobro.
I njuh mu kao starcu nije najbolji.
Lepo leži na podu, na rukavicama,
a nedaleko od peći gde gore drva.
Ponekad legne na ledja i okrene
prema nama svoj beli trbuščić.
Voli da ga mazimo po glavi
ili po gustoj dlaci ispod brade.
Noćas je prespavao u dvorištu,
na otvoru koji ide iz podruma.
Od njega bi ljudi mogli da uče.
Žilav je, izdržljiv, nije agresivan.
Mudro i dostojanstveno dolazi
do onoga što baš stvarno želi.

The Adopted |

The tomcat, Darwin, has adopted us.
That portly and wise vagrant
has chosen to spend his time with us,
and even sleep in this house on occasion.
I'm sorry for that street cat,
and feed him several times per day.
His head and ears are covered with scars.
Most likely, the green-eyed stray doesn't see very well,
and his nose, like an old man's, doesn't work the best.
He lies on his paws on the floor
close to the stove where the wood fire is burning.
At times, he turns over on his back
and show us his white belly.
He loves to have his head scratched,
and the thick hair under his chin.
Last night he slept in the yard
at the entrance to the cellar.
People could learn things from him.
He's tough, persevering, but not aggressive.
Shrewdly and with dignity
he gets for himself what he truly wants.

Vidim ih gde sede na električnoj žici.
A crna žica rastegnuta je iznad ulice.
Dan je turoban, kišovit i nebo sivo.
Vidim ih pribijene jedno uz drugo.
Kiša im kvasi perje i tiho rominja.
Oni se jedva pokreću i svoje glave
ne okreću jedan prema drugom.
Da li ih spaja ljubav i greju li se?
Štite li se od hladnoće kišnih kapi?
Ne znam, samo primećujem tela
ovako pribijena jedno uz drugo.
Na toj crnoj i dosta debeloj žici
vidim dva siva ptičja stvorenja
uobličena u jedno jedino pitanje.
Kad sam opet napolje pogledao,
video sam praznu žicu sa koje su
oboje odjednom i naglo odleteli,
odlepršali, a ne znam kuda i zašto.

I watch them sitting on the electric wire
stretched black over our street.
It's a gloomy day, rainy, the sky is gray.
I see them pressed to each other.
The rain softly falls and wets their feathers.
They barely move their heads,
and never look at each other.
Is it love or warmth that keeps them close?
Are they shielding each other from cold raindrops?
I've no idea, I only note
the closeness of their bodies
on that black, thick wire,
two gray feathery beings
joined into a single question.
When next I happen to look outside,
I see the wire is empty,
as if they both suddenly took off flapping their wings,
god knows where or why.

Anzelm Kiefer | *Zvonku Makoviću*

U knjizi koju mi je dala crnokosa, crnooka
i uvek u crno odevena lepotica Olga, po ocu Nemica,
po majci Ruskinja, gledam crnobele fotografije
"crnoga" slikara, Bojsovog učenika, Anzelma Kifera.
Slikar je prkosno navukao dugački vojnički šinjel.
Na nogama ima jahaće čizme i stoji na ledu u kadi.
Kao Hrist kad hoda, on stoji na zaledjenoj vodi.
U polutami, led sija kao suncem obasjana činjenica.
U knjizi koju mi je dala crnooka, crnokosa, vitka Olga
vidim olovne avione, staklo, emulziju, crna i siva platna.
U knjizi je mnogo crnog na belom, baš kao u ovoj pesmi.
I mada iz crnog nesanice, iz nigreda, ili iz crnice možda
dolaze mnoga sunčana stvorenja, biljke i svetle stvari,
svim svojim moćima suprotstavljam se bićima tame,
crnom noćnih ptica, mračnoj lepljivosti gmizavaca,
gavranovoj i vraninoj tamnini, ledenoj boji ponoći,
podzemnoj tmini i ljudskoj zaslepljenosti i pomrčini.
Ali blistanje i energija ne dolaze samo odozgo, sa neba,
već i od sila zemlje i mada nas mitovi uče šta je prvo,
a šta poslednje, jedino obožavam sile vazduha, vode, vatre
i ženskog tela i samo se njihovim jarkim bojama opijam.
U knjizi koja preda mnom leži naga, kao što crni hleb
na seljačkom stolu leži dok čeka nož da ga preseče,
u toj knjizi vidim tragove vremena, slamu, pesak, olovo,
Sefirote i kosu Sulamit, izgorelo žutilo leta izobilja.
Ali šta vidim iza slika, šta vidim iza opipljivih stvari?
Šta vidim u Kiferovoj knjizi "Herojski simboli"?

Anselm Kiefer | *for Zvonko Makovic*

In the book given to me by the black-haired, black-eyed
and always dressed in black Olga, whose father was German
and mother Russian, I study the black and white photographs
of "the black" painter, Beuys's pupil, Anselm Kiefer.
The painter has defiantly put on a long military coat.
On his feet he wears riding boots as he stands in an iced-over tub.
Like Christ when he sets out, he stands on frozen water.
In the half-darkness, the ice glows as if lit by the sun.
In the book given to me by the black-eyed, black-haired, slender Olga,
I see planes made out of lead, black and gray canvasses, glass,
    emulsions.
In the book there's a lot of black on white as there is in this poem.
And although out of black sleeplessness, nigredo, or out of black earth
perhaps come many sunlit beings, plants and bright things,
with all my powers I fight against the creature of darkness,
the blackness of night birds, the dark stickiness of reptiles,
the crow's and raven's darkness, the icy color of midnight,
the darkness under the earth, human blindness and obscurity.
But light and energy don't only come from above, from heaven,
but from the forces of the earth. And though myths teach us
what comes first and last, I only adore the powers of air, water, fire
and that of a woman's body, and with their bright colors I intoxicate
    myself.
In the book which lies before me naked, like black bread
on a peasant's table waiting for the knife to cut into it,
I see traces of time, straw, sand, lead, Sephirot and
the hair of Shulamite, the burnt yellow of a rich summer.
What do I see beyond the paintings, what do I see between
    what can be seen?
What do I see in Kiefer's book "Heroic Symbols"?

Možda konačnu istinu i stvarnu boju Nemačke?
Nešto oštro i lepo kao kod Kaspara Davida Fridriha?
Uništavanje, vaskrsavanje iz pepela i ruševina?
Zastrašujući red i čistoću, užasnu graničnu crtu
između pećinskog crnila i alpske beline?

Perhaps the real truth and the true color of Germany?
Something sharp and beautiful as in Caspar David Friedrich?
Destruction, resurrection out of ashes and ruins?
Frightening order, and cleanliness with its terrifying fine line
between the cave-like blackness and the Alpine white?

Svemoćna prijateljice beline noći,
hajde da se pomirimo i nagodimo.
Znam, po mene ćeš na kraju doći.

Ali pre toga, nemoj me više mučiti,
nemoj mi dosadjivati i okolo kružiti
kao crna mačka oko nevinog mesa.

Predugo smo jedno drugo hranili,
dugo sam ti žrtvovao sve divote
koje su mi nebo i zemlja poklonili.

Neka mi preostale dane i noćne tmine
ispune vedre igre, smejanja i radosti.
Neka sunce Mediterana na mene sine.

A kad mi zakreštiš, kad me pozoveš,
u crno ću zaroniti, pa iz njega izroniti
da me belinom mlečnog mlaza nazoveš.

Almighty friend of white night,
Let us make peace and come to an agreement.
I know you'll come for me in the end.

But before, don't make me suffer any more,
don't bother me and circle around me
like a black cat around innocent meat.

Too long we've fed each other,
too long I sacrificed to you every pleasure
the earth and the sky have given me.

Let my remaining days and nights
be filled with laughter and joy.
Let Mediterranean sun shine on me.

And when you caw to summon me,
I'll dive into blackness and then burst out of it,
so that you'll compare me to gushing milk.

PART III

74

Sada meko uranjaš u popodnevnu tišinu.
Ruka si što ulazi u zečje krzno rukavice.
Golotinja si što glatko klizne da zaiskri
medju tamnim pokrivačima od pamuka.
Senke se izdužuju i ribizlasto dozrevaju.
Iza ljubičastih zavesa u zagušljivim sobama
avganistanski tepisi upijaju polumrak i korake.
Na pletenim stolicama počivaju mrtve prirode.
Mrke doge tiho reže i zidni satovi odbijaju.
Rubini prstenja na dnu srebrnih škrinja
ne isijavaju čak ni boju vinskoga taloga.
Sve je to samo iluzija, samo kič i onanija.
Fijuke sečiva finskih noževa zamenjuješ
u ćumezima pored železničkih stanica,
zamenjuješ ih za milovanja kože nadlanica.
Ali isparavanja eteričnih ulja pretvaraš
u mirise tek ubranih i oljuštenih jabuka.
Pa ipak si patina svećnjaka i bakrenjaka.
Zato iz Berlina u desetleću posle Velikoga rata,
iz ruganja čudovišta, iz Grosovih njuški svinja,
iz Sutinovih impasta boje rasporenog govečeta,
iz Ensorovih pastoznih a iscerenih maski,
iz alkoholnih delirijuma, iz kokainskih snova,
prelaziš u tišinu, u lazurnu nostalgiju beskraja.
Ulaziš u hladno, u zagonetku jesenjej popodneva.
Meko uranjaš u nepokretnost, u popodnevnu tišinu.
A tvoji koraci čuju se na drugom kraju grada.
I devojčica svoj točak kotrlja u nepokretnosti,
ispod zelenog neba, kao i do sada, kao i do sada.

You rise early into the afternoon silence.
You are a hand entering a glove of rabbit fur.
Your nakedness slides easily and sparkles   75
among dark cotton covers.
Shadows lengthen as currants ripen.
Behind violet curtains in stuffy rooms
carpets from Afghanistan absorb the half-darkness and steps.
On a wicker chair still lives repose.
Brown mastiffs growl softly and wall clocks tick,
Ruby rings on the bottom of silver chests
can't match the color of dregs in a wine glass.
All is illusion, kitsch and self-gratification.
You swap the whistle of sharp Finnish knives
in dives next to the railroad station
for the stroking of the skin on your wrist.
The vapors of ethereal oils you convert
into scent of freshly picked and peeled apples.
Still, you're the patina of candlesticks and copper coins.
That's why from Berlin, in the decade after the Great War,
from jeering monsters, from Grosz's pig snouts,
from Soutine's impasto colors of the slashed open calf,
from Ensor's live-painted and leering masks,
from alcoholic deliriums and cocaine dreams,
you cross over into silence, into languid nostalgia for the infinite.
You enter the cold, the enigma of a winter afternoon.
You rise softly into the stillness, the afternoon silence.
Your steps can be heard on the other side of town,
while the girl rolls her hoop without moving
under the green sky as before, as before.

Nekada si mi ipak bila potrebna
da mirnije radim to što mi je dato.
Danas si obruč moje odbačenosti.
Usred tebe bivam lišen sposobnosti
dobrog kretanja, govorenja i gutanja.
Ukotvljujem se jedino u gledanju
stvari i bića oko sebe a ono u meni
nejasno je kao oblak jutarnje magle.
A jesi li možda predigra ništavila?
Mesto pre koga se gusto roje nule?
Jesi li i ti posed svemoćne Gospodje?
Ili samo deo beline o kojoj govorim
dok uveliko posvuda vlada ponoć,
gusta ponoć koja neće da prodje?

Once you were necessary to me,
so I could do what I had to do peacefully.
Today, you are the prison of my infirmity.
Within you I'm stripped of my abilities,
normal movement, speech, ability to swallow.
I'm reduced to watching things and other forms of life
around me while what is within me
is as blurred as a cloud of morning mist.
Are you, perhaps, a prologue to nothingness?
The place where zeroes swarm thickly?
Are you the estate of the all-powerful Lady?
Or only a bit of pale light of which I speak
while everywhere midnight reigns,
thick midnight that won't blow over?

Prošao mi je još jedan dan.
Duvao je vetar, navlačili se
oblaci, sunce izmedju njih sijalo.
Izašao sam u baštu i skupljao
osušene grančice koje su pale
sa drveta oraha kao žrtve vetra.
Nekada nisam verovao u sudbinu.
Danas sve više tonem u njenoj vodi.
Zanimaju me kamenje, trave, kiše,
snegovi, šume, vatre, morski talasi.
I još hiljade malih i velikih stvari.
Ali tu sam veoma čvrsto prikovan
kao za zid i za kratki gvozdeni lanac.
I idem samo do svoga bliskog zida
jer jedino to svojim telom mogu.
Daleko su mi beskraj ili večnost.
Vidim stvari što ih mogu opipati.
I sa njima i u njihovoj senci živim.
Znam, sudbina je reč koja se teško,
veoma teško u stvarnost pretvara.

Another day has passed.
Wind blew, clouds gathered,
the sun shone between them.

I went out into the garden
and gathered the dry twigs
the wind brought down out of a chestnut tree.
There was a time I didn't believe in fate.
Today, I'm drowning in it.
I'm curious about stones, grasses, rains,
snows, woods, fires and sea waves,
and hundreds of other small and large things,
while being chained securely to this wall
by a short iron chain.
Infinity and eternity are beyond my reach
since this is all my body allows me.
I see things I can touch,
and live with them in their shadow.
I know that fate is a word that with difficulty,
only with difficulty becomes reality.

Ponestalo nam je drva za loženje.
A ipak je još uvek je vreme hladno.
Uradio sam nešto što me ne raduje.
Uzimam svoju prvu knjigu poezije,
uzimam SA OBE STRANE KOŽE,
da, donosimo je iz podruma, iz paketa
vadimo je i tim knjigama belih korica
ložimo žutu kaljevu i crnu metalnu peć.
Spaljujem knjigu koju sam davno napisao
i sve me to podseća na druga spaljivanja,
na mnoga okrutna spaljivanja u istoriji
ali i paljenja knjiga u dvadesetom veku.
Knjigama dodajem i književne časopise.
Ali, ljudi, spaljujem samo svoje knjige.
Od tog papira sa rečima ostaje puno pepela.
Peći se zagrevaju od plamena papira knjiga.
Toplije nam je i možda se primičemo proleću,
sijanju sunca, toplom vremenu i vedrini neba.
A možda će nam ova spaljivanja ipak oprostiti
oni strogi i sve sudije koje treba da nam oproste?
Ali baš se, evo, pitam, ima li to spaljivanje knjiga
opravdanje, hoće li me zbog toga gristi savest?
Treba li se ipak žrtvovati u svemu i do kraja?
Smrzavanje u hladnom domu možda, prijatelji,
nije nešto čemu se treba ovako suprotstavljati
i spaljivati knjige, reči, rečenice, belinu hartije
a od njih dobijati crni, sivi pepeo i malo topline.

Book Burning |

We are out of wood to heat the house,
and still the weather is cold.
I did something that did not make me happy.
My first book of poems,
ON BOTH SIDES OF THE SKIN,
yes, we brought the copies up from the cellar,
took them out of the packages they were wrapped in,
and threw them in the yellow tile stove
and the black metal one. I'm burning books
I wrote a long time ago and doing so remember
other burnings, the many cruel ones in history,
and especially the ones in the twentieth century.
To my books I add literary magazines.
Listen, people, it's just my books I'm burning!
From the paper covered with words many ashes remain.
The stove heats up from the pages in flames.
We feel warmer and perhaps closer to spring,
the sun shining, balmy weather, clear skies.
Perhaps, we'll be forgiven for this fire
by the stern judges whose forgiveness we seek?
Nevertheless, I ask myself, is there an excuse for this,
Will my conscience bother me because of what I've done?
Should one sacrifice in everything for higher things?
Perhaps, friends, freezing in a cold house
is not something one should resist in this way
and burn books, words, sentences, white paper
and get from them black and gray ashes and a little warmth.

82

Dragi moj gospodine Slučaju,
ti što nas spasavaš ili nas kobno
pretvaraš u dosta drugačije ljude,
molim te, igraču, kaži mi, kaži
šta da radim i kuda da krenem?
Koji je onaj jedini ali moj put?
Kroz kakve ušice da se udenem?
Znam da baš ne voliš da pričaš.
A ni nežnost ti nije neka vrlina.
Brz si, ćutljiv i jako si probirljiv.
Je li naš odnos kao onaj oca i sina?
Ali, molim te, sažali se na mene!
Odgovori ili mi pokaži pravi put!
Sada sam poput neke jadne bene.
Eto, ne umem drugo da ti kažem.
Ali nisam nimalo i ni na koga ljut.
Danas te ovako tek usrdno molim,
uvaženi i dragi gospodine Slučaju.
A ako mi baš nikako ne odgovoriš,
tada za postavljanje važnog pitanja
preostaje mi da odaberem drugog.
Možda nekog bližeg samom kraju.
Nekog poput zemlje Severa golog.
Nekog ko je više sneg nego toplina.
Nekog ko svoju krv nalazi u očaju.
Možda je to ona svemoćna Gospodja?
Možda neko bodljikavo i ledeno biće

My dear Mr. Accident,
you who rescue us or fatally change us
into a very different person,
I pray to you, gambler, tell me, please,
what shall I do, where shall I go?
Which is my one and only path?
Through what eyelet should I thread myself?
I know you don't like to talk.
Nor is tenderness one of your virtues.
You are quick, taciturn and fussy.
Is our relationship that of father to his son?
Come, I beg you, take pity on me!
Answer me and show me the true way!
Now I'm like a poor simpleton.
There, I don't know how to tell you anything else.
Though I'm not in the least angry at anyone.
Today, I sincerely appeal to you,
dear, esteemed, Mr. Accident.
If you insist on not answering me,
then I have no choice but to choose someone else
to ask my important question.
Perhaps, someone closer to the end of his life.
Someone naked like the earth in the North.
Someone who is more snow than warmth.
Someone whose blood is despair.
Perhaps that someone is the almighty Lady?
A prickly and frozen creature

na koje vrane krešte i samotni psi laju.
Njihovi putevi idu daleko od svetlosti
tamo gde baš ništa i nikako ne sviće,
gde najčešće odlaze gospođjice Kosti.
I gde retko vidjamo devojke i mladiće.

at whom crows caw and lonely dogs bark.
Their road leads far from the light,
there where the day just won't break,
where mademoiselles Bones most often go.
And where we rarely see young men and women.

86

Doživeli smo najcrnje dane,
žena govori bez imalo žara.
Biće gorih dana i većih užasa,
mirno joj muškarac odgovara.
Uz njih dvoje ni vatra da plane.
Ali daleko im je konačni mrak.
Jedu beli hleb ili grizu jabuke,
piju ledenu vodu i zure u Ništa
što se primiče korak po korak
kao iz mrtvog mora grozni rak.

We've lived through darkest of days,
the woman says without any emotion.
Worst days are coming and greater horrors,
the man answers her quietly.
Next to them, not even a fire is lit.
Their final darkness is still far off.
They eat white bread and bite into apples,
drink cold water and stare at Nothing
that comes their way, step by step,
like a monstrous crab out of the Dead Sea.

88

Plavičasta oštrica ureže se u njenu koru
kao krik galeba u nepokretnost vazduha
iznad puste plaže, gde suše se mrke alge.

A prsti mi obnaže tu narandžastu svetiljku,
da mirisom Krita ozari mrak moje sobe,
kao kad sveža voda poškropi suvu biljku.

Like the cry of a seagull in the still air
above the empty beach where dark algae are drying,
The bluish blade cuts into her skin.   89

My fingers bare the nakedness of the orange lamp
so that with a scent of Crete it may light my room,
the way fresh water sprinkles a dry plant.

90

Pozdravljam te, Fernando Nogeiro,
pozdravljam te kao čovek koji zna
da se posle otvaranja jednih vrata
pred njim sva ostala vrata zatvaraju.

Pozdravljam te kao onaj koji zna
da posle svakog uplovljavanja u luku
dolaze novi odlasci i nove plovidbe
koje jedino smrt može da zaustavi.

A smrt je prava plovidba bez kraja
i možda konačno spasenje od svega.
Mrak ne možeš plavetnilom izbrisati.
Pomrčina ima bezbroj oblika i lica.

Pozdravljam te, Fernando Pesoa,
žudeo si za tolikim dalekim lukama
i plovidbama a ostao u Lisabonu,
želeći sve a dobijajući veliko Ništa.

Vrata okeana stvarno su najveća.
Pored njih stalno koračam i sedim.
Pored njih udišem isparenja algi
i čekam da nemi okean progovori.

Raspori sanjivo telo, tamni okeane,
ti džinovska životinjo plave krvi,
da onaj što je uvek pred vratima
u tebe udje i odmah vedro zaplovi!

Tako će mu ono daleko postati blisko.
Tako će se stopiti sa tvojom krvlju,
sa belinom talasa i sa prostranstvom
gde se izmiruju uzvišeno i nisko.

I greet you, Fernando Nogeiro,
I greet you as a man who knows
that when one door opens,
all other doors close to us.

I greet you as the one who knows
that after the return to the home port
come new departures and new journeys
which only death can put a stop to.

Since death is a journey that has no end,
and perhaps a final rescue from everything.
We cannot erase darkness with blue skies.
Darkness has too many forms and appearances.

I greet you, Fernando Pessoa.
You yearned for sea voyages and so many distant ports
while remaining in Lisbon, desiring all
and getting the Great Nothing in return.

The doors of the ocean are indeed the biggest.
 Next to them, I'm always walking and sitting.
Next to them I breathe the drying algae,
and wait for the dumb ocean to speak.

Dark ocean, you immense, blue-blooded animal,
slit open your sleepy body
for the one who is always before your door,
waiting to enter and cheerfully sail away.

So that what is far becomes near to him.
So that he becomes one with your blood,
with the whiteness of your waves and your breadth
where the exalted and the lowly make peace.

Oblaci Toskane, oblaci Umbrije,
beličasti oblaci što su vas slikali
Pjero dela Frančeska i Belini,

oblaci što vedro prolazite
dok ovde prolazim kao i svi,
putujem i plovim ka smrti,

razvedrite me vašom belinom,
tišinu mi razorite vašom grmljavinom,
i krv mi kišom probudite iz sna

da jasno vidim pomračeno juče,
bučno danas i bezglasno sutra
u ponoru bez vrha i bez dna.

Clouds of Tuscany, clouds of Umbria.
Pale white clouds painted by
Piero della Francesca and Bellini.

Clouds in clear sky passing by
while like everyone else
I sail toward my death,

cheer me up with your whiteness,
disrupt my silence with your thunder,
wake my blood with your rain,

so I can clearly see the dark yesterday,
the noisy today, the voiceless tomorrow
in an abyss without a top or bottom.

O, gundelji i prema vama sam bio zao.
Vi ste leteli i zujali kroz moje detinjstvo.
Ali hvatao sam vas i nabadao na drvca.
Njih sam potom u meku zemlju zabadao.
Iz braon tela curila vam je zelenožuta sluz.
Gundelji, vama sam se toliko, toliko radovao.
Vaše letenje najavljivalo je boje i lepotu leta.
Prema vama, mrka krilata bića, bio sam zao.
Spopada me kajanje zbog zla koja sam činio.
Možda je ono samo jednostavnost zbog koje
patim sada ili je sve samo slučaj što mi pruža
ova planeta, utočište leda zime i vreline leta?
Planeta gde su možda isto prosta kravlja muža
ili čovečija seta ili ime, meso puža ili silueta,
ova planeta gde se zlo i dobrota istim hrane.
A isti im je kraj, ista gusta, crna i bela meta,
isti cilj padanja lake a beličaste pene i mane.

O, flying beetles, toward you too I was mean.
You flew and buzzed through my childhood.
and I caught you and pierced you with a small stick
and then stuck you into the soft earth
till yellow-green fluid flew out of your brown bodies.
Flying beetles, I was so happy to see you.
Your flight presaged the beautiful colors of summer.
Toward you, dark flying beings, I was mean.
Now I feel remorse for the evil I've done.
This is, perhaps, the reason I suffer today,
or is everything this earth offers me
with its winter cold and summer heat only an accident?
This earth on which, perhaps, the udder of a cow,
a man's name, melancholy, the flesh of a snail or a silhouette,
are equally simple, this earth on which
evil and goodness eat the same food.
Their end is the same, the same thick, black and white aim,
the same reason light foam and manna fall.

Kad god pogledam taj džepni sat, setim se tebe,
dugih prstiju tvojih lepih ruku što nisu slikale,
setim se tvoje sede kose i tamnoljubičastih usana.

Stisnute su bile, jer si prezirao sirovost i ružnoću
sveta zaslepljenih i okrutnika, slepara i fanatika,
a ćutanjem krio svoju nežnost i ranjivost deteta.

U vreme germanskih demona gladovao si u Nirnbergu
i s nama zatim godinama živeo poput odsutnika
ili kao jedan od tridesetšestorice pravednika.

Posle svega, iza tebe su ostali: izgubljena ćerka,
ovaj džepni sat i prašnjava mandolina bez žica.
Užasavao si se i "mora života i mora smrti,

duboko žudeo za snežnim visovima" i dalekim poljima
netaknutim plimama promene, a u našoj pustinji,
ispunjenoj okeanima, kontinentima i gradovima,
rekama, državama i ratovima, bio senka što drhti.

Whenever I look at that pocket watch, I remember you,
the long fingers of your beautiful hands of an artist who never painted,
remember your hair and dark purple lips.

Drawn tight, since you despised the crudeness and ugliness
      of this world
the blind and the merciless, the deceived and fanatical have made,
and with your silence concealed your tenderness and child-like
      vulnerability.

In the time of Germanic demons, you went hungry in Nuremberg
and then lived with us afterwards for many years
like an absentee, or like one of the thirty-six just men.

After all that, you left behind: a lost daughter,
this pocket watch and a dusty stringless mandolin.
You were horrified that *there must be life; there must be death.*

You yearned for snow-capped mountains and distant meadows
untroubled by the tides of change while in our desert
with its many oceans, continents and cities,
rivers, countries and wars, you were just a trembling shadow.

98

Ćerka mi je iz Bombaja donela poklon.
Zeleni jastučak pun svakojakih trava.
Tu su Maticaria camomila, Brassica nigra,
Cinamomum camphora, Menta arvensis,
Zingiber officianale, Nardastachys jatamansi.
Hladna su i oštra ova imena na latinskom jeziku.
Taj jastučić treba da stavim u jastuk kad spavam
i moj san će, kažu, biti mnogo čvršći i dublji.
Biće prožet mirisima ali i snagom ovih trava.
Travu u mom dvorištu sekle su oštre kose
ili su ih šišale električne i motorne kosilice.
Znam, trave završavaju kao žuti stogovi sena,
kao denjkovi ili kao iščupano veliko busenje.
Gledao sam stogove putujući ka lepom Čačku.
Gutaju ih vatre i pretvaraju u crno i sivi pepeo.
Možda smo i mi ljudi samo nekakvi strukovi trave
koje visoke povijaju i lelujaju vetrovi s juga i severa.
Ne ličimo na zeleno busenje ali i toga ima u nama.
Lekovite trave, travuljine iz kojih cure zeleni sokovi,
krv trave, krzna zemlje što kao da su nokte u tlo zarile,
vlati trave koje grickamo, kojima hranimo životinje,
trave Volta Vitmena, trave detinjstva, morske trave.
Nalik lelujanju u vazduhu ili razilaženju lakog dima.
Ono što gusto i trepljasto niče i buja u snovima.
Toliko slično njima kojima hranimo naše duše,
njima u kojima smo kao kamenje na dnu vode.

My daughter brought me a gift from Mumbai.
A green pillow full of different herbs.
There's Matricaria camomila, Brassica nigra,
Cinnamomum camphora, Mentha arvensis,
Zingiber officinale, Nardostachys jatamansi.
Cold and severe are their names in Latin tongue.
That pillow I'm supposed to put inside my pillow,
so that my sleep will be harder and deeper,
penetrated by the scent and power of these herbs.
The grass in my yard was cut with sharp scythes,
or it was sucked by gas or electric lawn mowers.
I know, grasses end up as yellow haystacks,
as bales, or pulled clumps of earth.
I watched haystacks traveling to beautiful Čačak.
Fires devour them and turn them into black and gray ashes.
Perhaps, we human are like stalks of grass
which the wind from the north and south bends
        as they grow high.
We don't look like green clumps,
though there's even that within us.
Medicinal herbs, wild grasses out of which green juices
        flow like blood,
stalks of grass we chew or feed to the animals,
the grasses of Walt Whitman, the grasses of childhood,
        sea grasses,
the fur of the earth that dug its claws in the soil.
Like the air shifting, light smoke dispersing.
What quivers and thickly sprouts and flourishes in dreams.
So like those we feed our souls with, dreams,
in which we are little stones on the water bottom.

100

Drago moje Ništa,
ljubavlju i rečima
jednako pokušavam
da ti udahnem život.
Od silnog udvaranja
postajem deo tebe.

Zanosno moje Ništa,
kćeri ljudske praznine,
sad bih da izdahneš
ali ti si mi neuništivo,
ti si baš nedodirljivo
kao sve izmišljeno.

Hoću li se možda tebe
jednog dana osloboditi?
Ili ću te duboko u sebi
kao nešto čudno kriti
a ti ćeš okolo radjati
čudovišta i sablasti?

I šaputaćeš iste priče,
pljuštaćeš po meni
istim crnim pepelom
i pustinjskim kišama
ali nećeš mi izbrisati
mrlje krvi detinjstva.

Moje milo i bezoblično,
ti beskrvno i bezbojno,

My dear Nothing,
with love and words
I keep trying
to breathe life into you.
With so much flirting,
I'm becoming a part of you.

My dreamy Nothing,
daughter of human nothingness,
I want you dead and gone,
but you are indestructible,
truly untouchable
like everything imagined.

Will I be free of you,
one day perhaps?
Or will I hide you deep within me
while all around me you give birth
to monsters and specters?

You'll whisper the same stories,
pour over me
the same black ashes
and desert rains
without erasing the bloodstains
of my childhood.

My sweet and formless,
bloodless and colorless,

ti moje najdraže Ništa,
kojim očima da gledam
da bih te stvarno video
i lik ti večno zapamtio.

best-loved Nothing,
with what eyes shall I look at you
to see you truly
and remember your face forever?

noćas će neko nekoga jebati

dok državnici pregovaraju

razvezuju čvorove na kravatama

dugim gaćama i zategnutim medjunarodnim situacijama

i krišom ispod stolova češu i protežu mlohave udove

noćas neko će skočiti sa desetog sprata

ostavivši u sudoperu kuhinjske krpe i neoprano posudje

neko će se baciti iz voza u pokretu

zaboravivši da za sobom zatvori i prozor i vrata

i biće promaja i pobačaja stotine mrtvih insekata

neko će kraj otvorenog frižidera plakati

gledajući zvezde glodati rebro praseta

lenji kaktus rascvetava se noćas u vrtu

a meni će se smučiti i to malo tropine života

što se poput crva sveždera skutrila na dnu čaše

zato ću čašu i prepuni noćni sud prevrnuti

staviću tampone u usta i uši u nos i oči

i prkosno ću sebi u krtičnjake mesa vikati

tako da me i gluvi čuju tako da im u glavama sve brenca i buči

prodrmaću glasom sve svoje kosti

protestovaću protiv ne znam ni ja čega

protiv zemljine teže i sveže štampanih korisnih laži

protiv svega u savršenom poretku dezodorisanog sveta

    koji ne postoji

protestovaću ja koji ne postojim u zemlji što ne postoji

i tako sve ne postojeći hladnim oružjem

nežno ubijam psa mačku kanarinca i ženu

spustim zavese na prozorima porazbijam sijalice

spalim nameštaj pustim da bojler

tonight someone will fuck someone
while statesmen negotiate
untie the knots on neckties long underwear
and tense international situations
while secretly they scratch their balls under the table
tonight someone will jump from the tenth floor
leaving in the washer dirty dishes and dish rags
someone will throw himself from a moving train
forgetting to shut the window and door behind him
there'll be a draft aborting hundreds of dead insects
someone will cry next to the open refrigerator
watching the stars while gnawing a pork rib
tonight the summer cactus will flower in the garden
and I will grow nauseous of that small manifestation of life
huddled like a carnivorous worm on the bottom of a glass
I'll tip over the glass and the piss pot
stuff my mouth, ears, nose and eyes with cotton
and shout into the molehill of my flesh stubbornly
so the deaf hear me so that their heads turn into a bell and a
        clapper
I'll make all my bones rattle with my voice
I'll protest against I-don't-even-know-what
against gravity and newly printed useful lies
against everything in a perfectly ordered deodorized world
        which doesn't exist
I who do not exist in a country that doesn't exist
and thus with my nonexistent cold weapons
I will tenderly kill the dog the cat the canary and the wife
lower the window curtains break the light bulbs
set the furniture on fire let the boiler

eksplodira i svuda prospem šamponsku penu
oteram komarce i muve i zid zdruzgam čekićem
telefoniram predsedniku vlade i poniznim glasom
zaželim napredak u karijeri
a potom se prodernjam: kretenu i obećam
da ću ga častiti otrovanim pićem
onda počupam električne kablove i isečem vene
i uveren da će otsad sve na dobro da krene svučem se
sebi kažem laku noć mirno legnem da spavam snatreći u stelji
kako kratkovidi bog svojim uvek dežurnim teleobjektivom
kiklopski zakrvavelim okom
konačno blagonaklono pilji i u mene i u mene

explode while I pour foam out of a bottle of shampoo
chase the mosquitoes and flies break the wall with a hammer
telephone the president and in a humble voice
wish him much success in his career
and follow that with shouts of idiot and a promise
that I'll treat him to a drink spiked with poison
then I'll rip up the electric cord and cut my veins
convinced that from now on everything will go well
I'll take my clothes off wish myself goodnight and lie down
     calmly
daydreaming in bed like a nearsighted god
with the TV always at the touch of his finger
its Cyclops' bloody eye staring down at him benevolently

108

Sećam se, bio si usahla jabuka sred leta,
plod koji su napustila i sanjiva božanstva.
Regent's Park beše oaza sočnoga, zelenoga,
park pravilnih crta, leja, potkresanih grmova,
aleja, ukroćenost ostriženih kvadrata trava,
rukama baštovana obuzdana mašta zelenila.
U tebi, sreo sam sićušnog crnca iz Mozambika.
U tebi, razgovarao sam sa pederastim portirom
iz studentskog svratišta puste ulice York Terrace.
U tebi, pogledala me je Meri, crna čarobnica,
da sam je odmah poželeo i gladan i žedan crnila
uronio u somalijski tamno i glatko obilje
zarobljeno oklopom njene purpurne haljine.
Sećam se podrhtavanja njenih svežih dojki.
One su mi govorile najopojnijim narečjem.
Sećam se ukusa vrelih kamičaka njenih usana
i medljanog, mekog jezika što je softly,
softly razgrtao pepeo i budio mi žeravicu.
U pabu sam tada pio mlako Guinness beer,
a u restoranu jeo bljutavo-slatki beans.
Lakonoga jara spalila je travu u Hajd parku.
Jahačice na belim konjima promicale su
medju stablima, pod krpama krošnji platana.
Tog avgusta 1973, godine nekadašnjoj imperiji
vrtoglavo je na berzama padala vrednost funte.
Ćaskao sam sa starcem, pijanim Poljakom,
nekadašnjim kuvarom, odrpancem u kaputu.
Ćaskao sam ispred prepune stanice Viktorija
i nudio ga mlekom koje je sa gnušanjem odbijao.
Jedne noći u podzemnoj železnici bio sam zaslepljen

I remember, you were an apple tree wilted in the middle of summer,
its fruit abandoned by the sleepy deities.
Regent's Park was an oasis of lusciousness and greenery,
a park of straight lines, flower beds and pruned bushes,
paths, the stiff mowed squares of grass,
the imagination of plants held back by the hand of the gardener.
There, I met a small black man from Mozambique.
There, I met the effeminate porter from the student's hostel
      on deserted York Terrace.
There Mary, the black sorceress, looked at me
so that I desired her immediately, hungry and thirsty for blackness
to dive into her Somalian darkness and smooth plentitude
concealed in the armor of her purple robe.
I remember the quavering of her young breasts.
They spoke to me in a most inspired dialect.
I recall the taste of hot pebbles on her lips,
and the honeydew tongue that softly, softly
stirred my ashes and roused my embers.
In a pub I drank the lukewarm Guinness,
In a restaurant ate the tasteless sweet beans.
Fleet-footed heat had burnt the grass in Hyde Park.
Women riding on white horses passed between tree trunks
under the ragged crowns of plane trees.
That August 1973, the anniversary of ex-empire,
the value of the pound fell steeply on the stock market.
I chatted with an old man, a drunk Pole,
an ex-cook, a bum in a tattered coat.
I chatted outside the crowded Victoria Station,
offering him milk, which he turned down with disgust.
One night in the underground I was blinded

bleskom svetlosti i spopala me je osama
tokom šetnje na kiši po Marylebone Road,
kraj odurnih, kraj avetinjski zjapećih prozora
zgradurine Kraljevske muzičke akademije.
A sada, sećam se izmagličastoga Tarnera
u Tejt galeriji i jagoda koje nisam brao.
Sećam se rasističkih izjava mojih prijatelja.
I vožnje crvenim polovnim automobilom
u pogrešnom pravcu, kraj Bakingemske palate,
oko Belgrejv skvera ili kraj dokova na Temzi.
Prošlost se podigla iz mraka kao neman iz talasa,
neman što sa sluzavih krljušti stresa dagnje, alge,
stresa moruzgve, otresa pesak, šljunak i dogadjaje.
Podigla se nezasita neman izgubljenog vremena.
Izronila je ta zbirka imena činjenica, Vitgenštajne.
Izronila mi je aleksandrijska biblioteka nežnosti.
Na dnevnoj svetlosti zatreperila je kao čestica prašine.
I rasprsla se kao imenica, ogledalo bačeno sa sprata.
I pretvorila se u grudvu snega što se iz nigdine
kao pas dokotrljala do mojih vrata, da bi se rasula
u halapljivom ždrelu sadašnjosti, da bi se istopila
od miline miholjskog leta, od slovenske topline
mojih srpskih glagola i svih glagolskih predaka
kao da nikada, stari krvniče, kao da nikada,
čini mi se, baš nikada nije ni postojala.

by a flash of light and overcome with loneliness
walking in the rain on Marylebone Road,
past the hideous, apparition-like, gaping windows
on the huge building of the Royal Academy of Music.
Even now, I remember the misty Turner
in the Tate Gallery and the strawberries which I didn't pick.
I remember the racist pronouncements of my friends,
and a ride in a red jalopy on the wrong side of the road
past Buckingham Palace, around Belgrave Square,
and along the docks on the Thames.
The past rose out of darkness like a monster out of the waves,
A monster who shakes muscle shells from his slimy scales,
shakes off algae, medusas, shakes off sand, gravel and events.
The insatiable monster of lost time rose.
The almanac of names and facts surfaced, oh Wittgenstein!
The Alexandrian library of tenderness came up.
In broad daylight a grain of dust flickered
and broke up like a noun, a mirror thrown from the second floor,
and changed into a snowball that out of nowhere,
like a dog, rolled to my door, to scatter
in the gluttonous belly of the present moment, to melt
in the sweetness of Indian summer, from the Slavic warmth
of my Serbian verbs and all my verbal ancestors,
as if never, old cutthroat, as if never,
or so it appears to me, it never even existed.